COOL COLOURS CAPTURE THE

The only thing that the pieces of furniture in this room have in common is a certain purity of line which is especially suited to the understated style of the patterns in this book. Look for pieces of furniture with straight, slender legs and a minimum of fussy mouldings. Many Edwardian pieces of no

great value, in dark wood or veneer, have a latent quality which our restrained treatment brings out brilliantly. Notice how the Ribbons and Bows colour scheme is keyed into the equally calm decoration of the room itself. Again painted in blue and cream, the walls play off the pale blue beneath the dado rail

MOOD OF A MOMENT

against the broad stripes of blue and cream above. Use emulsion paint and masking tape to ensure the crisp, straight lines on which the elegant effect depends. The unified colour scheme and absence of fuss make for a spacious, classy effect which anyone could copy and feel comfortable with, for the

Gustavian style is essentially unpretentious. A Swedish house of the period might well stand its painted furniture on bare boards of scrubbed pine, and restrict soft furnishings, as here, to a simple fall of muslin at the window and rustic checks for cushions and chair covers.

PAINTING WITH A PATTERN

With the help of our pull-out patterns and transfer paper, even absolute beginners can learn how to handle a range of motifs, from the simplest leaf-and-berry border to a fluttering rococo bow. Soon you will be able to create something as poised as the chair shown opposite.

Points to remember:
• Much of the delicacy and liveliness of the painted decoration shown here in close-up derives from the use throughout of artists' gouache dissolved in gum arabic, both materials obtainable from any artists' suppliers.
• Gouache is a vivid and concentrated form of watercolour in tubes, popular with illustrators and graphic designers because it is much easier to handle than the classic type of watercolour pan (or block) sold in tin sets that everyone remembers from childhood.
• Gum arabic, a clear fluid, makes an excellent, controllable, transparent paint when tinted with gouache, adding fluency to brushwork and offering a wide range of tone - the more gouache you add to the gum arabic, the stronger and less transparent the colour.
• Only a few gouache colours were used to paint our motifs, the subtle tonalities being achieved simply by varying the dilution of gouache colours in gum arabic.
• Soft watercolour brushes, in sizes from medium to fine, are essential for a neat finish. But there is no need to buy expensive sable brushes - synthetic bristle or mixed hair are fine.

1 THE SIMPLE LEAF-AND-BERRY MOTIF, OFTEN SEEN AROUND THE RIM OF A VASE, IS FIRST TRACED DOWN WITH A SHARP PENCIL ABOVE A PIECE OF BLUE TRANSFER PAPER, CUT TO FIT FOR CONVENIENCE.

2 WITH THE TRANSFER PAPER LIFTED OFF, THE SIMPLICITY OF OUR TRACE-DOWN METHOD OF DECORATION IS CLEAR TO SEE.

3 USING A MEDIUM-FINE BRUSH DIPPED INTO COLOUR A, THE BASIC LEAF SHAPES ARE PAINTED IN. USE THE BRUSH TO CREATE DEPTH BY INCREASING PRESSURE AT THE FATTEST POINT OF THE LEAF. YOU MAY NEED TO PRACTISE THIS FIRST ON A PIECE OF PAPER.

5 USING COLOUR B (AND DILUTING THE GOUACHE COLOUR QUITE HEAVILY WITH GUM ARABIC) DARKER STROKES ARE ADDED TO THE UNDERSIDES OF THE LEAVES AND TO ONE SIDE OF THE BERRY SHAPES.

6 COLOUR C IS THEN APPLIED AS SHOWN TO CREATE HIGHLIGHTS ON THE OPPOSITE SIDE OF THE LEAF AND BERRY SHAPES.

7 RETURNING TO COLOUR B, THE DARK SHADING IS FILLED OUT AND EMPHASIZED FOR A SIMPLE THREE-DIMENSIONAL EFFECT. FINALLY, USE COLOUR C TO HIGHLIGHT THE DETAILS OF THE MOTIF.

MATERIALS CHECKLIST

WELL-SHARPENED HARD LEAD PENCIL, SCISSORS,
MASKING TAPE, OLD PLATE FOR USE AS A PALETTE,
WATER JAR, KITCHEN PAPER OR TISSUES, RULER OR
TAPE FOR POSITIONING MOTIFS, SPRAY VARNISH.
TUBES OF GOUACHE PAINTS IN ULTRAMARINE,
PERMANENT GREEN DEEP, RAW SIENNA, RED OCHRE
AND FLAKE WHITE.
SMALL BOTTLE OF GUM ARABIC FOR DILUTING
GOUACHE COLOURS.
WATERCOLOUR BRUSHES FROM MEDIUM TO FINE.

NOTE: Transparent watercolour paint
is inherently more fragile than
emulsion and needs 'fixing' on
completion of decoration, *before* you
proceed to further varnishing,
antiquing etc. All the decoration in
this series was fixed with a rapid
blast of spray varnish, available from
artists' suppliers.

4 THE SAME BRUSH IS NEXT USED TO 'BLOB'
IN THE ROUND BERRIES THAT ALTERNATE
WITH THE LEAVES, STRENGTHENING THE VISUAL
IMPACT OF THE STALK.

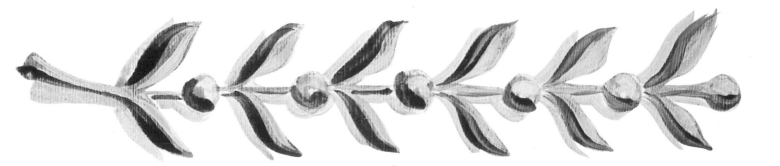

THE COMPLETED BORDER SHOWS HOW ARTFUL
BRUSHWORK AND A CONTROLLED USE OF
TONES, FROM LIGHT TO DARK, CAN MAKE A
VIVID LITTLE PASSAGE OF DECORATION FROM
THE SIMPLEST OF SHAPES.

COLOUR RECIPES
A ULTRAMARINE PLUS PERMANENT GREEN DEEP
B MORE ULTRAMARINE THAN A
C A PLUS FLAKE WHITE

The casual bow of ribbon with its fluttering ends and nonchalant grace is one of the timeless charmers of the ornamental repertoire. It is - or was - also notoriously testing to paint, but the step-by-step instructions for our trace-down bow make this versatile motif accessible to anyone who has mastered the techniques set out on the preceding pages.

1 THE BOW IS BUILT UP USING THE SAME TECHNIQUE OF SHADING FROM LIGHT TO DARK AS APPLIED FOR THE LEAF-AND-BERRY BORDER; BUT HERE THE BRUSHWORK IS MORE TENTATIVE, BEING COMPOSED OF SHORT STACCATO STROKES.

2 COLOUR B, THE DEEPEST TONE, IS SUPERIMPOSED OVER THE BASIC SHAPE (IN COLOUR A) USING THE FATTEST BRUSH IN A LOOSER MOVEMENT. IT SHOULD FEEL ALMOST AS IF YOU ARE LETTING THE BRUSH FIND ITS OWN WAY.

5 THE COMPLETED BOW DEFINES ITS FRAGILE DELICACY BY NOTHING MORE THAN THE CAREFUL GRADATIONS OF TONE AND AN OVERALL LIGHTNESS OF EXECUTION.

3 COLOUR C, THE LIGHTEST BLUE-GREEN TONE, HIGHLIGHTS SECTIONS OF RIBBON IN IMITATION OF LIGHT FALLING ON A REFLECTIVE FABRIC SUCH AS SATIN, SILK OR MOIRÉ.

4 THE SAME PALER TONE IS NOW USED TO 'FATTEN UP' SECTIONS OF THE BOW. THIS BACK-AND-FORTH STYLE IS NECESSARY BECAUSE EACH NEW STEP REQUIRES A NEW RESPONSE.

1 DIFFERENT SITUATIONS DEMAND DIFFERENT BOWS. THIS MORE PENDANT VERSION IS GOOD FOR CENTRING A BEDHEAD OR A PELMET, AND SERVES AS AN ANCHOR FOR ORNAMENT.

2 THE DEEPEST TONE, COLOUR B, GIVES DEPTH, EXPRESSION AND SHADING TO THE BASIC MID-TONE BOW SHAPE.

3 THE FINISHED BOW HAS TRAILING RIBBONS PAINTED IN COLOURS A AND B FOR A LIGHT BUT VIVID PRESENCE.

1 THE EXQUISITE PENDANT AND SWAG MOTIF IS COMPOSED OF REPEATED BELLFLOWERS. HERE THE BELLFLOWERS ARE BEING FILLED IN USING COLOUR A (AS USED FOR PREVIOUS PATTERNS).

2 THIS SHOWS THE COMPLETED MOTIF USING ONLY THE BASIC MID-TONE, COLOUR A. TRY TO KEEP THE PRESSURE THE SAME ON THE LEFT AND RIGHT SIDES OF THE MOTIF.

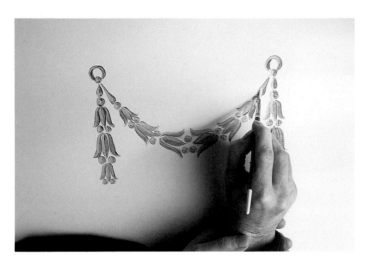

3 A DEEPER TONE, COLOUR B, IS USED TO INTENSIFY AND DRAMATIZE THE MOTIF BY SHADING AREAS AS SHOWN.

4 HIGHLIGHT THE SIDE OPPOSITE THE SHADED AREAS USING THE MID-TONE LIGHTENED WITH FLAKE WHITE (COLOUR C).

5 FINAL TOUCHES ARE ADDED, IN COLOURS B AND C, TO STRENGTHEN THE WHOLE MOTIF AND GIVE IT VIVACITY.

6 THE COMPLETED DESIGN HAS AN ELEGANCE AND LIGHTNESS OF TOUCH THAT EVEN ROBERT ADAM WOULD HAVE APPRECIATED.

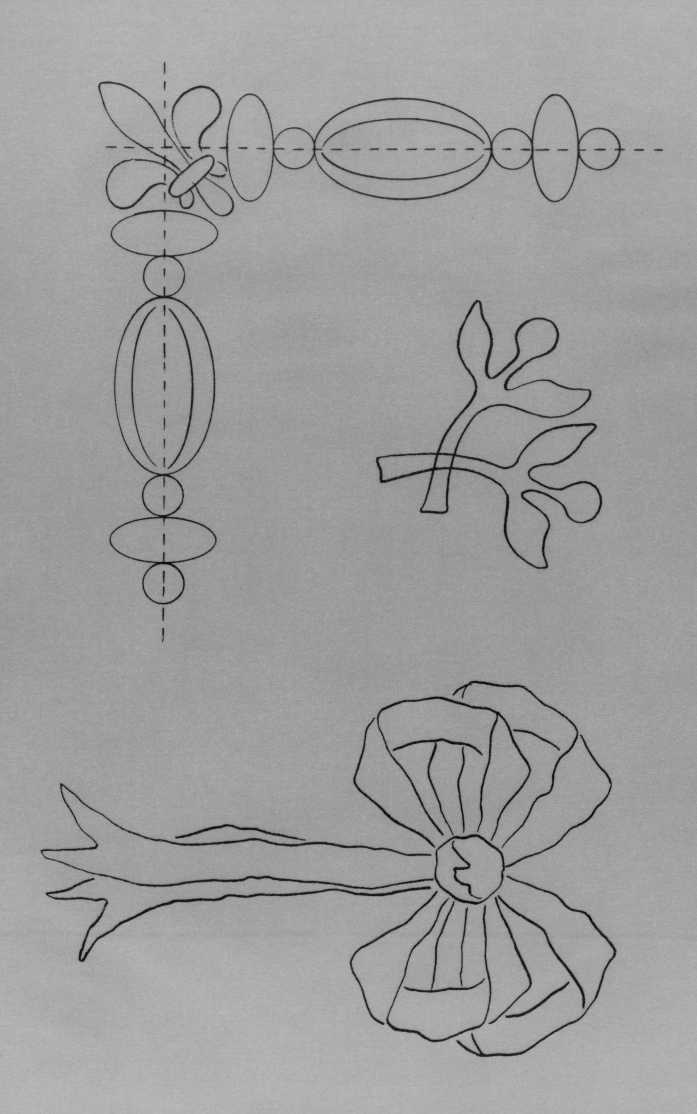

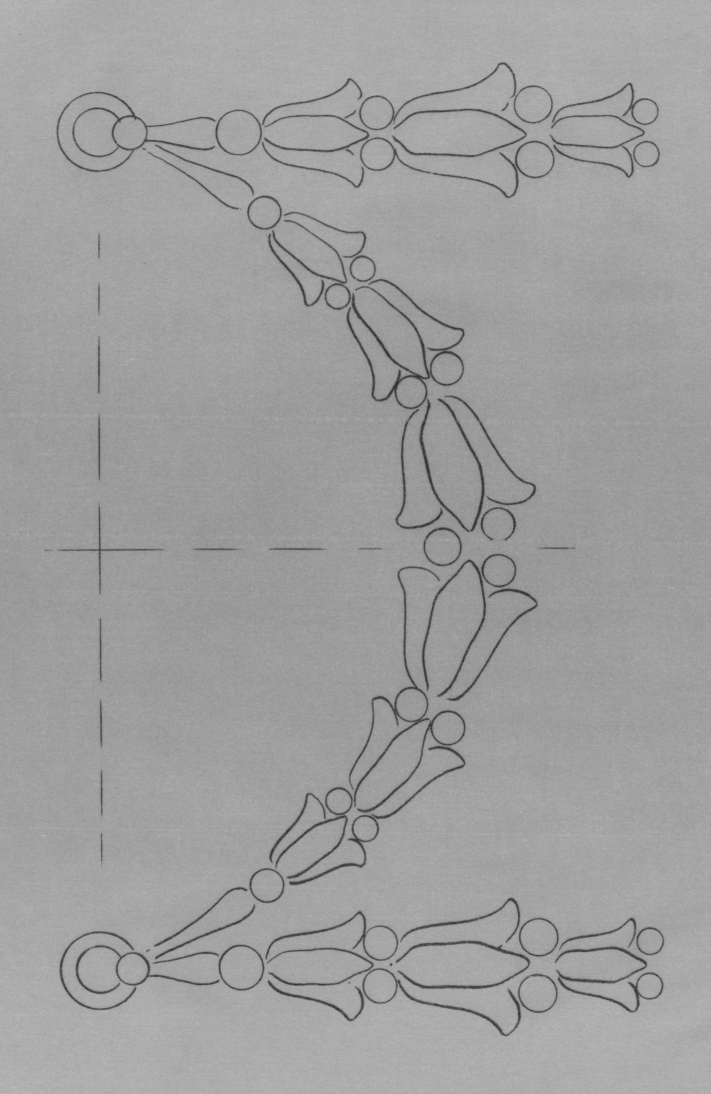

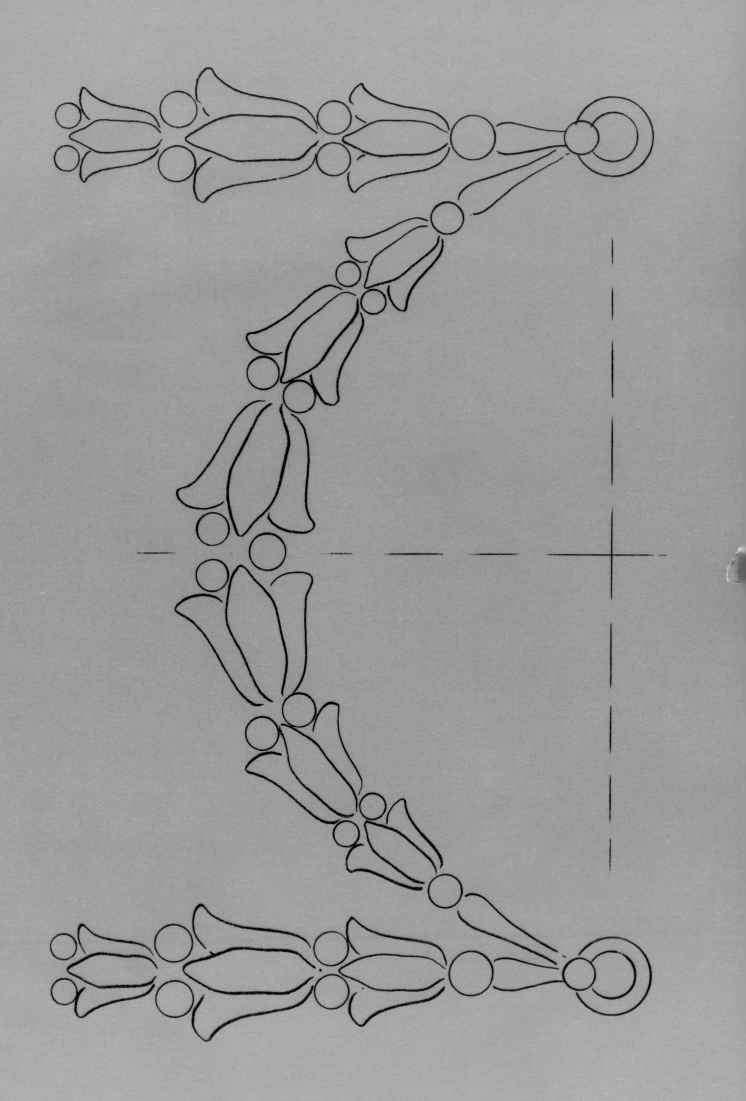

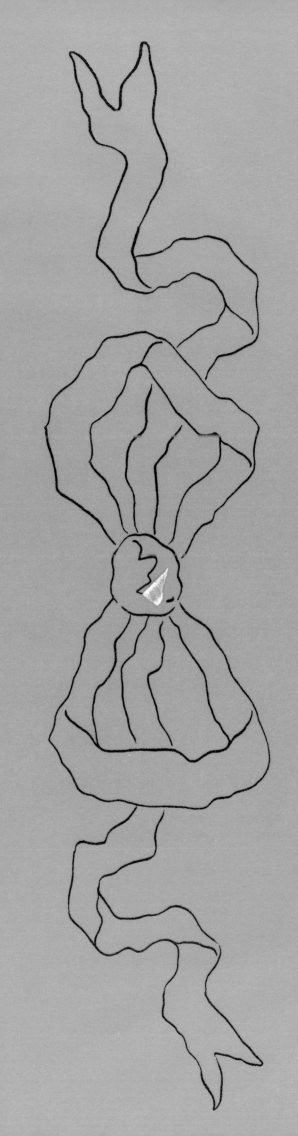

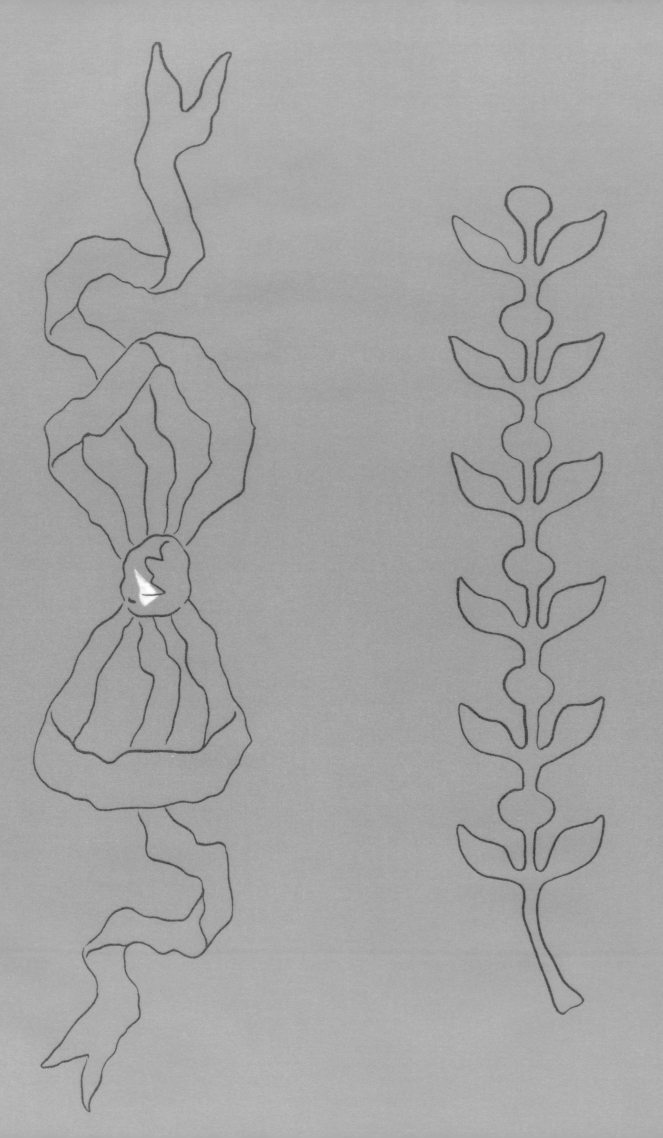

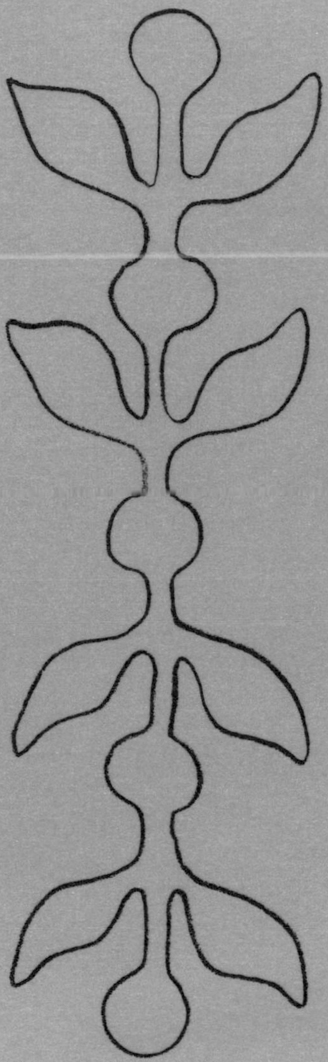

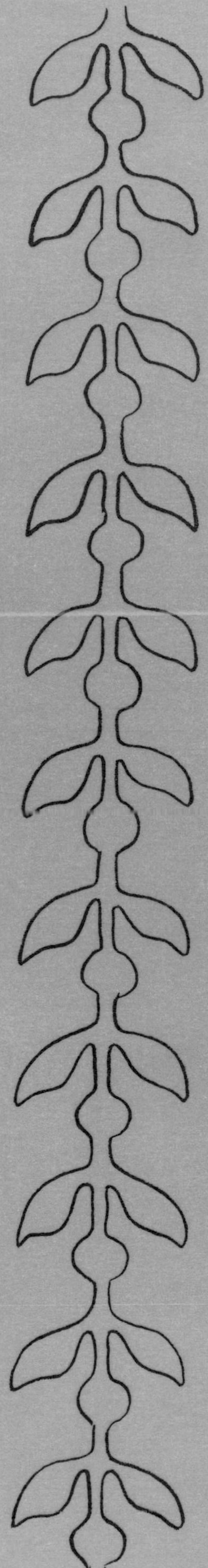

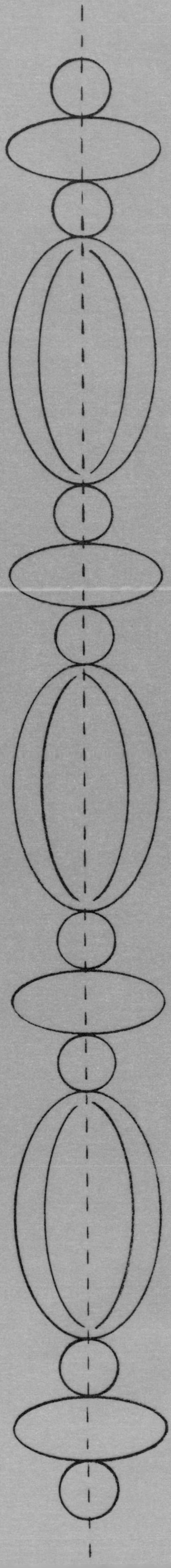

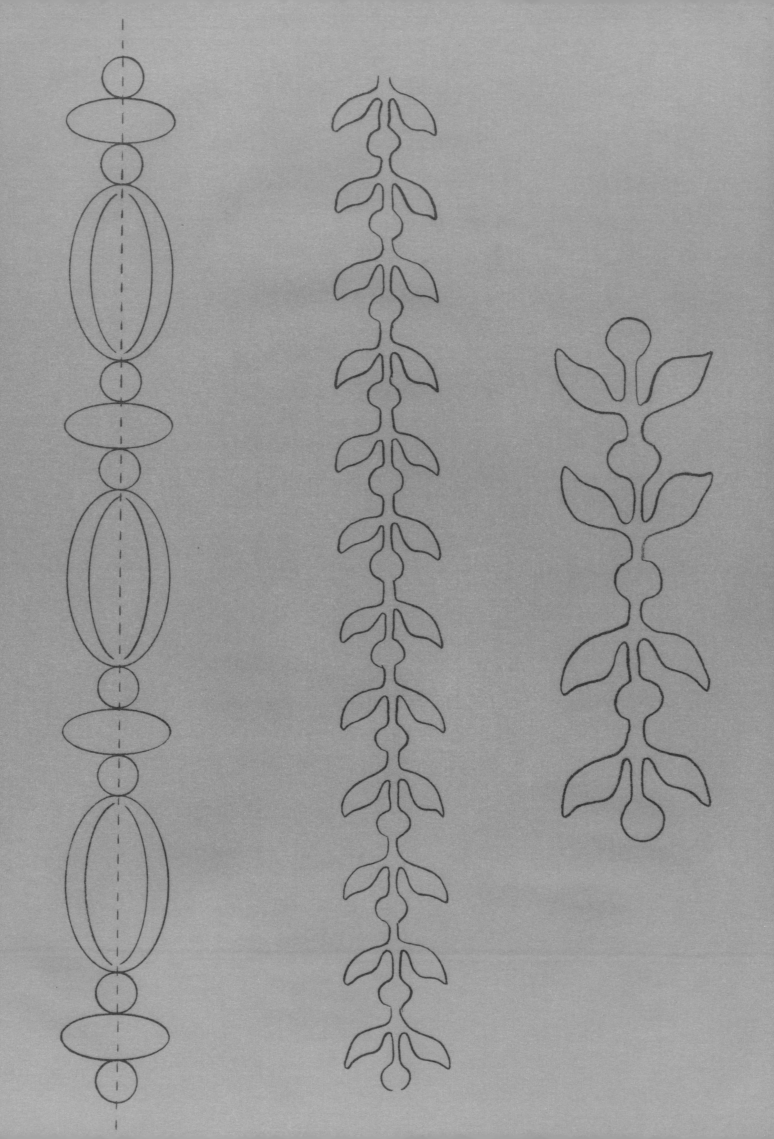

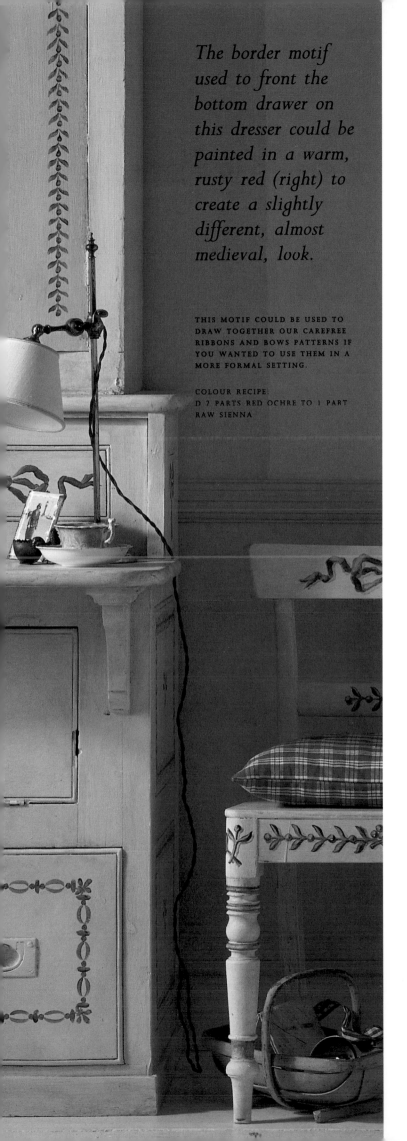

The border motif used to front the bottom drawer on this dresser could be painted in a warm, rusty red (right) to create a slightly different, almost medieval, look.

THIS MOTIF COULD BE USED TO DRAW TOGETHER OUR CAREFREE RIBBONS AND BOWS PATTERNS IF YOU WANTED TO USE THEM IN A MORE FORMAL SETTING.

COLOUR RECIPE:
D 7 PARTS RED OCHRE TO 1 PART RAW SIENNA

1 NOTICE HOW THE CORNER MOTIF FOR THIS BORDER PATTERN IS ACCURATELY ALIGNED WITH THE SECTION OF TRACED-DOWN BORDER SHOWN HERE FOR A NEAT EFFECT.

2 USE A MEDIUM BRUSH AND COLOUR D TO PAINT IN THE ROUNDED BARREL SHAPES USING THREE STROKES FOR EACH ONE. USE A BLOB OF PAINT FOR THE DOTS BETWEEN THE BARREL SHAPES.

3 WITH A SLIGHTLY DEEPER TONE OF THE SAME COLOUR (THAT IS, WITH A LITTLE MORE GOUACHE ADDED TO THE FORMULA) THE SHAPES ARE ENRICHED AND LIGHTLY SHADED FOR EMPHASIS.

DECORATIVE DETAILS CAPTURE THE CHARM

The right finish adds warmth and character to our suite of Ribbons and Bows.

Like the rest of the Ribbons and Bows furniture, this attractive bedside cupboard was base-painted in an ivory matt emulsion over acrylic primer. Afterwards, the watercolour decoration was applied and 'fixed' with spray varnish, and then the entire piece was given two final coats of protective varnish, each with a little colour added to lend a subtle warmth and age to the colour scheme and to make the ornament 'lie down' and blend harmoniously.

THIS CLOSE-UP DETAIL OF OUR BE-SWAGGED WINDOW SEAT SHOWS HOW THE INITIAL COLDNESS OF THE IVORY BASE HAS BEEN GIVEN A GOLDEN TINGE BY APPLYING A LIGHTLY TINTED VARNISH. USE A GOOD-QUALITY MATT VARNISH OR A MID-SHEEN POLYURETHANE FOR HEAVY-DUTY PROTECTION. REMEMBER THAT THESE ARE OIL-BASED, SO TINTING SHOULD BE DONE WITH A LITTLE ARTISTS' OIL TUBE COLOUR (RED OCHRE OR RAW SIENNA) DISSOLVED IN A LITTLE WHITE SPIRIT. STIR THIS INTO SOME DECANTED VARNISH, MIX WELL, AND THEN TEST IT FIRST ON AN INVISIBLE PATCH.

A whole package of bright ideas tied up with our Ribbons and Bows.

Once you have hit upon a winning theme like this one, it is an exciting challenge to think of new uses for the basic motifs. The beauty of traditional ornament is that it never looks dated or over the top. Designers have endlessly recombined these same pattern elements over the centuries, and the ideas shown here only hint at the range of possibilities.

WHEN IS A TRAY NOT A TRAY? WHEN THE ADDITION OF PAINTED CHEQUERS AND A LITTLE CUPBOARD BENEATH TURNS IT INTO A HANDY GAMES TABLE, WITH SPACE TO STORE THE PIECES AND OTHER PARAPHERNALIA. THE DISCREET PLACING OF OUR RIBBONS AND BOWS MOTIFS LIFTS A JUNK DUO INTO AN ELEGANT LITTLE PIECE THAT WOULD LOOK RIGHT AT HOME JUST ABOUT ANYWHERE.

THE PENDANT BOW PREVIOUSLY USED TO FILL IN A SMALL VERTICAL PANEL ON A BUREAU FINDS A NEW LEASE OF LIFE S-T-R-E-T-C-H-E-D AND PAINTED STRAIGHT ON TO THE WALL AS A VISUAL LINK FOR A FAVOURITE COLLECTION OF BLUE-AND-WHITE CHINA PLATES. THIS PRETTY IDEA LOOKS MORE EFFECTIVE WHEN PAINTED THAN IT WOULD WITH ANY REAL RIBBON.

STRIPED WALLS HAVE AN EIGHTEENTH-CENTURY FORMALITY, BUT ARE GIVEN A TWENTIETH-CENTURY LOOK HERE BY USING BROAD STRIPES OF MATT EMULSION PAINTED DIRECTLY ON TO THE PLASTER. USE A PLUMB LINE AND MASKING TAPE AS A GUIDE TO PAINTING THE STRIPES NEATLY.

THE LEAF-AND-BERRY BORDER IS ENOUGH TO LEND A CRISP NEW STYLE TO A VERY ORDINARY WOODEN TRAY. NOTE HOW THE MOTIF IS ARRANGED FOR SYMMETRY ON A LONG BORDER, WITH A CENTRAL BERRY AND THE BORDER GOING IN OPPOSITE DIRECTIONS EITHER SIDE. FOR GREATER DEFINITION, QUITE WIDE 'RULES' WERE ADDED ON THE BASE AND AROUND THE TOP, USING THE SAME TRANSPARENT WATERCOLOUR APPLIED FREE-HAND WITH A WATERCOLOUR BRUSH. ALTERNATIVELY, YOU MIGHT FIND THIS EASIER TO DO WITH A LONG BRISTLED LINING BRUSH, OR WITH MASKING TAPE TO DEFINE THE 'RULES'. BUT A FREE-HAND LINE WITH A SLIGHT WOBBLE ALWAYS LOOKS BETTER THAN ONE DONE WITH MASKING TAPE WHEN IT'S ON A SMALL SCALE SUCH AS HERE.

The long, dark winters have taught the Scandinavians to hoard any available natural light, choosing pale colours everywhere and using filmy muslin for curtains. Gutsier colour and contrast are introduced with traditional fabrics, flowers, candles and other details.

THE PHOTOCOPIER MAKES QUICK WORK OF ALTERING THE SCALE OF ANY OF OUR DESIGNS, EITHER ENLARGING OR REDUCING THEM TO SUIT A PARTICULAR SPACE. HERE, FOR INSTANCE, THE BOW HAS BEEN REDUCED A LITTLE TO FIT NEATLY INTO A DRAWER FRONT, WHILE THE SWAG AND PENDANTS HAVE BEEN CLEVERLY ARRANGED TO MAKE A FEATURE OF THE CENTRAL DRAWER KNOB BELOW.

THE SAME BOW AS ON THE DRAWER FRONT, BUT LARGER THIS TIME, ADOPTS A NEW ROLE BINDING UP THREE SPRAYS CREATED FROM LENGTHS OF LEAF-AND-BERRY. NOTE THE THREE LITTLE 'TAILS' BENEATH THE KNOT OF THE BOW, WHICH WERE ADDED FREE-HAND TO BALANCE THE COMPOSITION. OFTEN A LITTLE DETAIL IS ALL YOU NEED TO MAKE SOMETHING QUITE NEW FROM THE SAME MOTIFS.

SWAGS AND PENDANTS WERE OFTEN USED TO ENCIRCLE ROUND TABLE TOPS. THEY ARE IDEAL PATTERNS TO APPLY CONTINUOUSLY AROUND A CURVED SHAPE, EVEN WHEN THE 'CURVES' ARE ANGLED AS ON THIS UNUSUAL WINDOW SEAT. THE IMPORTANT THING IS TO CENTRE THE FIRST SWAG IN THE MIDDLE OF THE FRONT SPACE - THIS IS THE STARTING POINT FOR ANY SYMMETRICAL USE OF ORNAMENT.